THE NATURE KIDS GUIDE TO
PARROTS

DAVID ANDERSON

LP Media Inc. Publishing
Text copyright © 2026 by LP Media Inc.

For information address LP Media Inc. Publishing,
30012 Variolite St NW, Princeton MN 55371
www.lpmedia.org

Publication Data

Parrots
The Nature Kid's Guide to Parrots — First edition.

Summary: "Learn all about Parrots, the Nature Kid Way"
— Provided by publisher.

ISBN: 979-8-89818-096-6

[1. Parrots – Non-Fiction] I. Title.

Title: The Nature Kid's Guide to Parrots

CONTENTS

TROPICAL TREES

Squawk! A bright parrot sits in a tree. Its colorful feathers shine.

Parrots live in warm places around the world. These colorful birds need trees to live and raise their babies. Tropical forests give them food and safe homes.

Parrots eat fruits, nuts, and seeds from forest trees. Their strong beaks help them crack open hard shells. Some parrots also eat flowers and leaves.

The tropical forest is a busy place for parrots! They call to each other with loud sounds. Parrots often live in groups called flocks. They help each other find food and stay safe from danger.

PARROT PLACES

Screech! A green parrot flies over a misty forest.

Parrots live on many continents. Most live in South America, Australia, and Africa. Some also live in Central America and Asia.

These parrots like different kinds of homes. Some live in thick rainforests. Others live in dry grasslands or mountain areas.

A few parrots live in cooler places. The kea parrot lives in snowy mountains in New Zealand.

In Australia, some parrots dig underground burrows to nest in instead of living in trees.

BIG OR SMALL

Chirp! A Blue-and-yellow Macaw parrot sits on a hand. Some parrots are huge!

Parrots come in many sizes. Some are very big. Others are very small.

A hyacinth macaw can grow up to 40 inches long. Its wings stretch up to 5 feet wide when it flies. That's as wide as your bed!

The pygmy parrot is one of the smallest parrots. It is only about 3 inches long. This tiny bird weighs less than half an ounce!

The kakapo is the heaviest parrot. It can weigh up to 9 pounds. It cannot fly!

BRILLIANT BEAKS

Crunch! A red parrot bites into a hard nut. Its strong beak cracks it open.

Parrots have special beaks. Their beaks are curved and strong. The top part hooks over the bottom part.

A parrot's beak never stops growing. Chewing on wood and nuts wears it down to the right size. This also keeps the beak sharp.

Parrots use their beaks like hands. They can hold food and even climb branches. Some parrots also use their beaks to dig holes in trees for nests!

Parrots can crack nuts with 500 pounds of pressure; enough to snap a broomstick!

SUPER
SENSES

Click! A parrot turns its head. It hears a tiny sound.

Parrots have amazing senses. Their eyes can see **ultaviolet** light. This allows them to see secret colors and patterns that humans cannot see!

Parrot eyes sit on the sides of their heads. This helps them watch for danger all around. Each eye can move on its own.

Parrots hear very well too. They can hear sounds from far away.

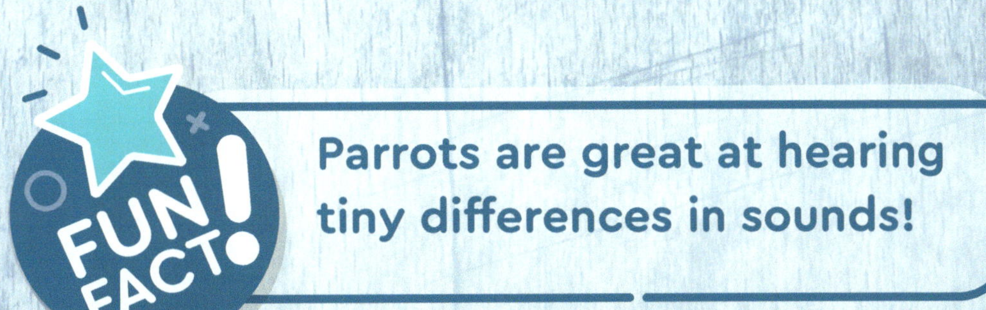

BOLD
COLORS
14

Snap! A blue and gold macaw spreads its wings wide.

Many parrots have bold, bright colors. Their feathers can be red, blue, yellow, or green. Some parrots have five, six, or seven colors at once!

Bright colors help parrots in the wild. In a leafy forest, colorful feathers can blend in with flowers and fruits.

Scientists think bold colors help parrots know each other. Each type of parrot has its own color pattern.

FUN FACT!

The rainbow lorikeet has feathers in almost every color of the rainbow.

NUTTY
SNACKS

Chomp! A Nanday Parakeet eats a seed. Now it looks for more food.

Parrots eat many kinds of food. They love seeds, nuts, and fruits. Some parrots also eat flowers and leaves.

Different parrots like different foods. Lorikeets drink nectar from flowers. Macaws eat clay from riverbanks!

Parrots search for food in trees. They use their feet to hold food while eating. Wild parrots spend hours finding meals each day.

Macaws eat clay to help digest poisonous seeds!

18

Squawk! A parrot calls out from a tree branch.

Parrots are some of the best talkers in the animal world. They can copy human words and sounds. Some parrots learn over one hundred words!

Parrots use their thick tongues to make sounds. They move air through a special body part called a **syrinx**. This helps them make different noises.

Wild parrots use calls to find their flock. They screech to warn about danger. Each flock has its own special sounds.

Baby parrots learn calls from their parents, just like human babies learn words.

WATCH OUT
20

Swoosh! A hawk dives toward a parrot. The parrot must escape fast.

Parrots face many dangers in the wild. Hawks and eagles hunt them from the sky. Snakes climb trees to find parrot nests.

Monkeys also eat parrot eggs and chicks. Big cats like ocelots catch parrots too. These hunters are always looking for food.

Parrots must stay alert to survive. They watch for danger all day long. Living in **flocks** helps them spot predators quickly.

Some snakes unhinge their jaws to swallow a whole parrot egg in one gulp.

FLY AWAY

Whoosh! A flock of parrots zoom through the trees to escape danger.

Parrots can escape predators by flying away quickly. Their strong wings help them move through forests.

Their bright colors also help them hide. The colors blend with flowers and leaves. This makes them hard to see.

Some parrots fly in zigzags too. This confuses predators chasing them. All these tricks keep parrots safe.

Some parrots fly up to 35 miles per hour and make sharp turns to escape hawks.

WINGS UP

Rustle! A parrot hops along a branch. It lifts its wings.

Parrots have strong wings for flying. These wings help them soar through the sky.

Some parrots have long pointed wing feathers. These help them fly fast. Others have shorter rounded wings.

Parrots flap their wings to take off. They can also glide through the air. Gliding saves energy on long trips.

Some parrots migrate over 1,800 miles each year, crossing mountains and deserts to find food.

BUSY BIRDS

Thump! A parrot lands on a perch. It starts to preen.

Parrots stay busy all day long. They wake up early in the morning. Then they start looking for food.

Parrots spend hours eating and drinking. They also clean their feathers often. This is called preening.

In the afternoon, many parrots rest. They take naps in shady spots. At sunset, they fly back to their sleeping trees.

Parrots yawn when tired, just like humans. They stretch one wing at a time before sleep.

FLOCK
FRIENDS

Buzz! Many parrots gather in one tree. They call to each other.

Parrots live in groups called flocks. A flock can have just a few birds. Some flocks have hundreds of parrots.

Parrots in flocks help each other. They warn about danger. They also find food together.

Flocks are noisy places. During the day, parrots squawk and chatter. Each parrot has its own special call.

Some parrot flocks sleep together in the same trees every night. These spots are called roosts.

FINDING
LOVE

Two parrots sit close together. They touch beaks softly.

Parrot pairs may stay together for many years. They sit close and preen each other to show love. Preening means they clean each other's feathers gently.

When it is time to raise a family, parrots make nests in tree holes. The female lays eggs inside. Both parents sit on the eggs to keep them warm.

Most parrots nest once a year, often during rainy season.

Male parrots often dance, bob their heads, and fan their feathers to impress a female they like.

CUTE CHICKS

32

Peep! A tiny parrot chick hatches from its egg. A new life begins.

Parrot chicks hatch without feathers. They cannot see at first because their eyes stay closed for about two weeks.

The chicks are very small and weak. They depend on their parents for everything. The parents bring food to the nest many times each day.

As weeks pass, soft feathers start to grow. Many young parrots leave the nest around six to twelve weeks. They then learn to fly and find food on their own.

PROUD PARENTS

Squeak! A parent parrot feeds its hungry chick.

Parrot parents work hard. They take turns caring for their young. One parent stays with the chicks while the other finds food.

Parents feed chicks by bringing up soft food from their own stomachs. This makes it easy for babies to eat. They feed chicks many times each day.

Young parrots stay with their parents for months. They learn important skills like finding food. Some parrot families stay together for a whole year.

Some parrot parents teach their chicks special family calls.

PARROT
POWER
36

Squawk! A parrot glides through a steamy rainforest

Parrots are survivors. When people cut down forests, many animals disappear. But parrots often find ways to keep going.

These smart birds can learn to eat new foods. When their favorite fruits are gone, they find other things to eat, like seeds from backyard gardens or crops on farms.

Parrots also find new places to call home. Some now live in cities and suburbs. They build nests in palm trees, church steeples, and even holes in buildings

A group of monk parakeets built their nests on the cold, windy beaches of New York City!

PET PARROTS

Squawk! A parrot calls to its owner for food.

Parrots need care every day. Owners must give them fresh water and healthy food. Seeds, fruits, and vegetables keep parrots strong.

These birds need clean cages. Dirty cages can make parrots sick. Owners should clean the cage often.

Parrots also need time outside their cage. They like to play and stretch their wings. Toys help keep their minds busy.

Some parrots can live for 50 years or more. That is a very long time to care for a pet!

GLOSSARY

tropical
A warm place where it never gets cold and plants grow all year.

flocks
Groups of birds that live and fly together.

syrinx
A special body part in a bird's throat that lets it make sounds.

preening
When birds clean and fix their feathers with their beaks.

ultraviolet
A type of light that humans cannot see, but parrots can.